2 DESCRIPTION SIGNALEMENT

Bearer Titulaire	*Wife Femme	Bearer Titulaire

Profession / Profession: STUDENT Musician

Place and date of birth / Lieu et date de naissance: LIVERPOOL 9th OCT 1940

Country of Residence / Pays de Résidence: ENGLAND

Height / Taille: 5 ft. 11 in.

Colour of eyes / Couleur des yeux: HAZELBROWN

Colour of hair / Couleur des cheveux: BROWN

Special peculiarities / Signes particuliers:

*CHILDREN ENFANTS

Name Nom   Date of birth Date de nais...

---

2 DESCRIPTION SIGNALEMENT

Bearer Titulaire	Wife Femme	Bearer Titulaire

Profession / Profession: MUSICIAN

Place and date of birth / Lieu et date de naissance: LIVERPOOL 9/10/1940

Country of Residence / Pays de Résidence: ENGLAND.

Height / Taille:
ft. in.

---

2 DESCRIPTION SIGNALEMENT

Bearer Titulaire	Spouse Epousse	Bearer Titulaire

Occupation / Profession: MUSICIAN

Place of birth / Lieu de naissance: LIVERPOOL ENGLAND

Date of birth / Date de naissance: 9 OCTOBER 1940.

Residence / Résidence: U.S.A.

Height / Taille: 5 ft. 11 in.

Distinguishing marks / Signes particuliers: —

Spouse Epousse

Photo

CHILDREN ENFANTS

Name Nom	Date of birth Date de naissance	Sex Sexe
SEAN TARO ONO LENNON	9-10-1975	H.

LIFE

Remembering
John Lennon
25 Years Later

Above: **Liverpool, 1945**
Photographs by the Lennon family
© Apple Corps.

 Books

Editor Robert Andreas
Director of Photography Barbara Baker Burrows
Creative Director Ian Denning
Deputy Picture Editor Christina Lieberman
Writer-Reporters Hildegard Anderson (Chief),
Elizabeth Hoover
Copy Wendy Williams (Chief), Lesley Gaspar
Production Manager Michael Roseman
Assistant Production Managers Leenda Bonilla,
Rachel Hendrick
Photo Assistants Joshua Colow, Eirini Vourloumis
Picture Editor Suzanne Hodgart (London)
Consulting Picture Editors Mimi Murphy (Rome),
Tala Skari (Paris)

Editorial Director Robert Sullivan

President Andrew Blau
Business Manager Roger Adler
Business Development Manager Jeff Burak

Editorial Operations
Richard K. Prue (Director), Richard Shaffer
(Manager), Brian Fellows, Raphael Joa, Stanley E.
Moyse (Supervisors), Keith Aurelio, Charlotte Coco,
Erin Collity, Scott Dvorin, Kevin Hart, Rosalie Khan,
Marco Lau, Po Fung Ng, Barry Pribula, Albert Rufino,
David Spatz, Vaune Trachtman, David Weiner

Time Inc. Home Entertainment

Publisher Richard Fraiman
Executive Director, Marketing Services
Carol Pittard
Director, Retail & Special Sales Tom Mifsud
Marketing Director, Branded Businesses
Swati Rao
Director, New Product Development Peter Harper
Assistant Financial Director Steven Sandonato
Prepress Manager Emily Rabin
Book Production Manager Jonathan Polsky
Marketing Manager Laura Adam
Associate Prepress Manager
Anne-Michelle Gallero
Associate Marketing Manager Danielle Radano

Special thanks to Bozena Bannett, Alexandra Bliss,
Glenn Buonocore, Bernadette Corbie, Suzanne Janso,
Robert Marasco, Brooke McGuire, Stanley Parkes,
Chavaughn Raines, Ilene Schreider, Adriana Tierno

Published by **LIFE** Books

Time Inc. 1271 Avenue of the Americas,
New York, NY 10020

ISBN: 1-932994-23-8
Library of Congress Control Number: 2005906438
"LIFE" is a trademark of Time Inc.

We welcome your comments and suggestions about
LIFE Books. Please write to us at: LIFE Books, Attention:
Book Editors, PO Box 11016, Des Moines, IA 50336-1016

If you would like to order any of our hardcover Collector's
Edition books, please call us at 1-800-327-6388
(Monday through Friday, 7:00 a.m.–8:00 p.m., or Saturday,
7:00 a.m.–6:00 p.m., Central Time).

Please visit us, and sample past editions of LIFE,
at www.LIFE.com.

Classic images from the pages and covers of LIFE are now
available. Posters can be ordered at www.LIFEposters.com.

Fine-art prints from the LIFE Picture Collection and the LIFE
Gallery of Photography can be viewed at
www.LIFEphotographs.com.

Introduction

Rock 'n' roll was born kickin' and screamin' in America in the 1950s, as revolutionary sounds from Chuck Berry, Buddy Holly, the Everlys, Bo Diddley, Eddie Cochran, Jerry Lee Lewis, Little Richard, Elvis Presley and others commandeered the airwaves and blared defiantly from jukeboxes. Young people thrilled to a beat all their own, and kids in other parts of the world dug the music, too—and sometimes even tried to play it. But the only tunes that mattered—that were the real deal—came from the States.

The new music found an eager audience in Britain, as a dreary postwar climate left disenfranchised teenagers wanting something—anything—that was different. A lot of them keyed in to the American scene, and a few were ready and willing to pattern themselves after the American acts. But if they were ready and willing, these performers

were not so able, at least from a Yankee perspective. The likes of Tommy Steele and Cliff Richard were popular in the U.K., but to Americans, the few who heard them at all, these Brits were nothing more than wannabes. They lacked originality, and the true rock feel.

Luckily for the future of rock 'n' roll, there were others than Steele and Richard who were listening to the music. One of them was a bright if directionless boy in Liverpool who came alive at age 15 when he heard a recording by Elvis. Empowered, John Lennon, a middle-class child of confusion from Liverpool, formed a band, and therein took hold of himself. Before too long another young Liverpudlian, Paul McCartney, joined with him, and these anxious teenagers set about learning their craft.

By the early 1960s, though rock 'n' roll still ruled the musical roost, the lifeblood had been drained

On October 20, 1958, George Harrison's eldest brother, Harry, was married, and the Quarry Men— including Paul, John and George—were fortunate to play at the wedding reception at the Childwall Abbey Hotel in Liverpool. Whether they knew it or not, the guests were surely fortunate as well.

from the medium. Elvis had gone into the service, then had returned a little too grown-up, and more than a little too Hollywood. Chuck and Jerry Lee got entangled in scandals that took them out of the mix, and Little Richard, of all people, chose to devote himself to the spiritual rather than the secular. Rock, such as it was, had become the purview of white-bread teen idols, bland performers lip-synching bland numbers. Frankly, it seemed all was lost. But as we now know, this was not the case. Things were heating up in Merrie Olde England.

The fine American R&B singer Delbert McClinton was on the scene at the time, and tells LIFE, "In April 1962, about a year before the Beatles changed the world, I was playing harmonica with Bruce Channel—who had a hit at the time with 'Hey Baby'—at the Tower Ballroom in New Brighton. The Beatles were the opening act, and John Lennon came up to me and asked if I used a chromatic harp on 'Hey Baby.' We hit it off, and he came to the show we did in Liverpool and again in London, where he took me to an after-hours joint. We were both 22 years old and both had big plans to make our marks in life. John Lennon was the most charismatic person I had ever met."

Delbert is right: John defined charisma, and the Beatles did change the world. The music of the Fab Four swept over the globe like a wondrous tornado. Although it incorporated Elvis and Buddy and Chuck and the others, it was different from anything that had come before, and these particular Brits definitely had the real feel.

Of course, it was more than the music. When young people around the world got a look at the Fab Four, at their hair and clothing and the instinctively entertaining way they handled themselves, it was the beginning of a cultural sway unlike anything pop music had ever witnessed. John was the leader, although eventually the magnitude of the Beatles diffused any notion of a front man. They simply *were,* and young people everywhere followed them with rapture.

By 1970 the fury of the group proved too much, and the band's members went their own ways. It wasn't a pretty parting; the blinding pressures of interstellar popularity—even worship—would have undone any mortal team. By this time, John was completely taken with Yoko Ono, an avant-garde performance artist he had met in London in 1966.

John was a tough guy, at least on the outside, but he had met his match in Yoko. Together the two would lead a life alternately public and private, but nearly always together.

So it would remain until the end, an ending that was simply all too unfair. John's life for years had been devoted to nonviolence, and an unhappy person needed but a gun to take him from us. Fortunately we have our memories. There are the songs and the movies, and with this book a collection of pictures that will forever crystallize one of our greatest artists. Of special note are the sections devoted to six photographers who were there at critical times with the man, helping immortalize the one and only John Lennon. These individuals speak to us, exclusively, in these pages, thinking back 25 years and more. Their pictures speak to us, too—and ever will.

This portrait of John was taken just weeks before his death.

Allan Tannenbaum/Polaris

A Liverpool Lad

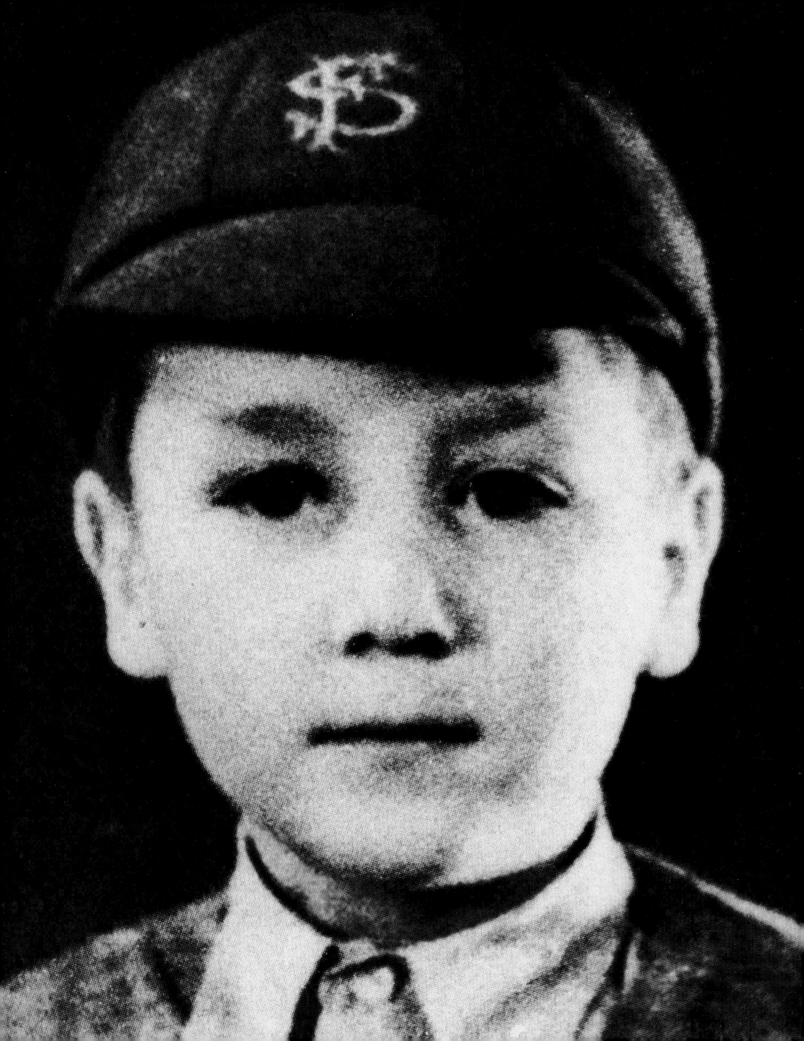

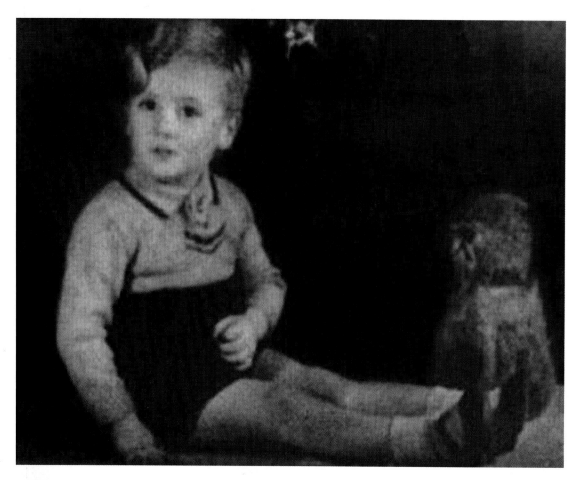

John and his elder cousin Stanley Parkes were good chums. Here, circa 1948, they are outside Aunt Mimi's house, "Mendips." At left, John in 1944.

Octtober 9, 1940. Bombs are falling on Britain as Germany is trying to blast the little nation into submission. Liverpool, an important port city in the northwest, has been taking a particular pounding. On this day, during a brief lull in the bombardment, a child is born at the Oxford Street Maternity Hospital. His name is John Winston Lennon.

John's father, Alfred, was away at sea, and would never have much of a part in his son's life. The mother, Julia, was temperamental, ill-prepared for raising a son on her own, and frankly not that interested in it. However, Julia's sister Mary Smith, better known as Mimi, was a different matter. She adored the boy; it was she who chose his name. With Julia out and about, Mimi and her husband, George, raised young John, who, desperate for attention, often ran the three miles from his home to their suburban house. When John was five years old, he finally moved in with them.

Mimi was loving, but she was also strict. Julia, on the other hand, now relieved of any disciplinary responsibilities, became a kind of carefree friend to John. She saw him fairly regularly, and it was she who taught him to play the banjo. Her son, understandably, developed complex feelings toward her that would haunt him after she was killed by a drunken driver when the boy was 17.

School was a problem. He skipped classes and was often in trouble. Aunt Mimi arranged for him to get into the Liverpool College of Art, but even this proved too regimented for him.

The lad was foundering, but there was a ray of light. In May 1956, a friend played Elvis Presley's "Heartbreak Hotel" for him. At long last a jolt of energy shot through Lennon. Here was something that called out to him . . . took hold of him . . . a feel . . . something that was on his wavelength . . . something that shook a lad who had been wandering in a daydream and made him feel, at once, alive. Relentlessly he begged Mimi to buy him a guitar. She did, saying, "The guitar's very well, John, but you'll never make a living out of it."

This was hardly the sort of advice that would sway a besotted teenager. Guitar in hand, John formed a band called the Quarry Men. They weren't very good, not at first, but lord knows, the lead Quarry Man had quite a future ahead.

Beloved Women

Above, in 1948, John poses (rather fitfully; he was all boy) with his mother, Julia. Opposite, about two years later, he is a bit more composed with Aunt Mimi. These two sisters were the most important people in the boy's life, but the other three Stanley sisters also had a hand. In a 1975 interview with *Playboy,* John said, "There were five women who were my family. Five strong, intelligent women. Five sisters. One happened to be my mother. My mother was the youngest. She just couldn't deal with life . . . Those women were fantastic." Even though he moved in with Mimi at age five, he continued to see his mum and would later write two haunting songs about her, "Julia" and "Mother."

Rex

"There Are Places I Remember . . ."

The extended family often got together on holidays. At left, circa 1949, John sits outside his cousin Stanley's house in Rock Ferry, across the Mersey, with (clockwise) his cousin Leila, half-sister Julia, cousin David and cousin Michael. Above, John (with arms spread) frolics on a school trip to the Isle of Man. Below, in the backyard at Mendips, John shows off a puppy recently given him by his uncle George. Unfortunately, a few weeks later Aunt Mimi broke John's heart by giving the dog away. Stanley told LIFE that Mimi disposed of the dog "because she was daft about cats."

John Lennon Museum/© Yoko Ono Lennon

David Birch

The Quarry Men

Elvis's "Heartbreak Hotel" had been the beacon in the night for John, but it was skiffle that made him want to form a band. Skiffle was an English music popularized by Lonnie Donegan that was part pop, part jug band. Here, at 16 years old, John is the lead singer for the Quarry Men, who are performing at a summer fete on a makeshift stage behind St. Peter's Parish Church. Apart from skiffle, the Quarry Men—whose name was taken from their high school, Quarry Bank—specialized in shifting personnel. On the day this picture was taken, July 6, 1957, there was a 15-year-old in the audience who was very taken with the group, and would soon add to the personnel changes by joining the band. His name was Paul McCartney.

Astrid Kirchherr *Remembers*

"All they had were little snapshots from home, so I took them to the fairground and posed them. They were perfect for my black-and-white photography, and with their leather rock-'n'-roll-boys look, the rusted-steel lorries out there were suited to their image. They had never really posed, so I had to touch their legs and put them the way I wanted them."

Everyone wanted to take pictures of the Beatles and, later, John and Yoko. But a few photographers were there at critical moments, and thereby gained an intimacy that allows their portfolios to stand, all these years later, as the definitive telling of those chapters. These images are essential to how we remember John Lennon and his times.

Six seminal chroniclers of Lennon's life—Astrid Kirchherr, Terry Spencer, Bob Whitaker, Bob Gruen, Allan Tannenbaum and Harry Benson—are alive and well, and talked with LIFE for this book. Their reminiscences are insightful, poignant, sometimes sentimental—and very often fun.

In 1960, Astrid was a bright young photographer based in Hamburg when she was introduced by her boyfriend, Klaus Voorman, to this British quintet, the Beatles (from left, Pete, George, John, Paul and Stu; opposite, George, Stu and John; above, Astrid with Ringo and John in 1963). "We were so amazed by their looks and music," she says. "They were jumping around with joy, asking questions about everything." John got a kick out of the band's ultrahip German fans the *Exis*—existentialists—and a mutual admiration society, with influences flowing both ways, quickly formed. Astrid and Stu fell in love, became engaged, and when the band returned to England after another stint in Hamburg in 1961, Sutcliffe stayed behind. He died of a brain hemorrhage in 1962.

" I felt that John was a sad person. He looked like a hard Teddy Boy, but he wasn't at all—he was a very soft, gentle person. He was lovely and honest, especially when Stuart [right, in background] died. He asked me to take his picture then in Stuart's studio [above]. He said a typical John thing—'If you want to die, do that. But if you want to live, get on with it.' He was a very honest friend, and that is why I loved him so much. "

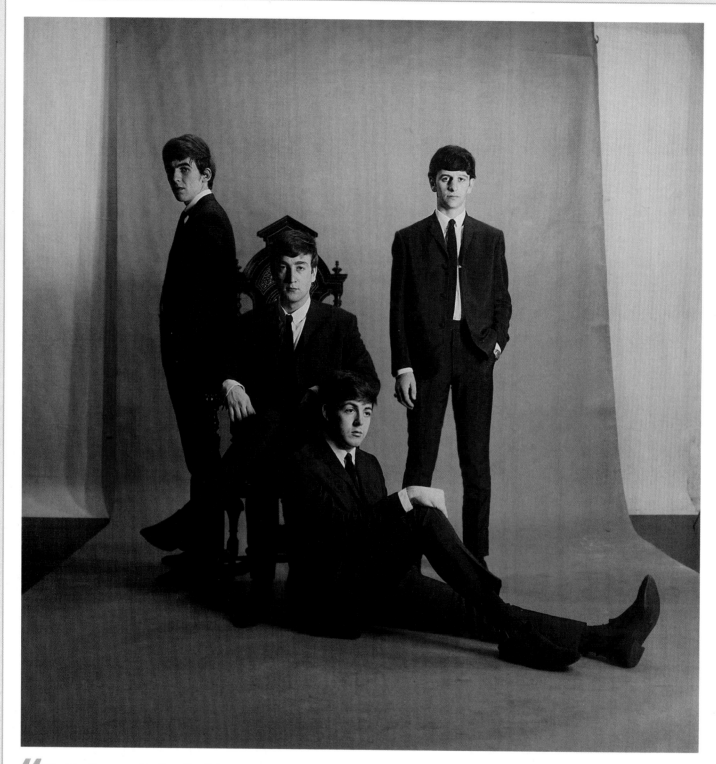

❝ The Beatles were the first English people I met, and you
must remember, this was not long after the war. We all learned
that these other people were not the enemies we believed
they were. We listened to one another. Yes, I gave Stuart the
haircut first—John made fun of it. But soon he wanted one, too,
and so did the others. The same haircuts or not, each of them
was strongly an individual. I could tell right away. **❞**

“ When it all took off in England, well, nobody could expect that sort of thing. But I did always feel that each one of them was going to succeed at something—Paul as a musician, John as a writer or cartoonist or whatever, Stuart as an actor or writer or painter. And then the Beatles happened for the four of them. At first, it still all seemed very innocent and actually pretty funny. ”

> John's legacy? His bravery. When he had the power, he used it. He really wanted peace on earth, and John's lyrics—well, that's the brave poetry of the '60s. If he had stayed with us, he could have done so much more.

Terence Spencer *Remembers*

In late 1963, the English photographer Terry Spencer had just returned home after a period of working for LIFE in various trouble spots around the world. He was met at the airport by his 13-year-old daughter, Cara, who gushed, "Dad, Dad, you've got to do a story on those fab Beatles!" Remembers Spencer: "As I'd never heard of them, my reaction was pretty much, 'Oh God, what's she on about now?'" He soon found out, and was able to chronicle the excitement as the first wave of Beatlemania swept across England and Europe. "All this was in 1963 and early '64," he tells LIFE. "I was in my forties at the time and was totally accepted by them. They trusted me implicitly, as I never tried to catch them unawares in bad moments. Of course, the mood was to change dramatically over the years, but in those early days they were essentially four very normal human beings who were always amusing themselves in the behind-stage bars, just having a lot of fun. They would tip me off to the little hotels they stayed in—they were mobbed in the larger ones—and I was able to join in with much of what they did, including going to Paris with them."

No one was more thrilled by Terry's whirlwind association with the Beatles than his daughter. "Once, in a bar in Manchester, I persuaded Lennon to make a short ditty for Cara on the tape recorder that I always carried with me to make captions," recalls Terry. "John said, 'Hello, Cara. How are you? We have your old man here buggering us around, following us everywhere.' Then he started off on the guitar, joined by Harrison and McCartney. Only after strong protest and foul language did he get Ringo to join in, tapping on the bar with his drumsticks while the others sang messages to Cara." Terry debated with his wife whether to give Cara a recording laced with vulgarities, and was told that there was nothing on the tape that Cara hadn't already heard from her dad's mouth. "Later," Terry continues, "when Cara went to play the tape for a friend for the umpteenth time, it was accidentally erased. It was a tragic day, with tears for many nights to come. "That I was later able to introduce her to the boys themselves did console her a little."

" John was the wittiest and also the most abrasive. 'People who think we had it easy can think again,' he said. 'Shortly before our big break, we had a good week when we made 20 pounds apiece and that was doing four shows a day.' He added: 'The day the fans desert us, I'll be wondering how to pay for my whiskey and cokes.' "

They didn't want to pose for shots, but that wasn't the kind of photograph I wanted anyway. I remember that, although they weren't at all conceited, they were quite self-conscious about their appearance. They used to sit in front of a long mirror—they always shared a dressing room—to do their hair and make themselves up. They used minimal makeup, just a little powder to offset the sweat.

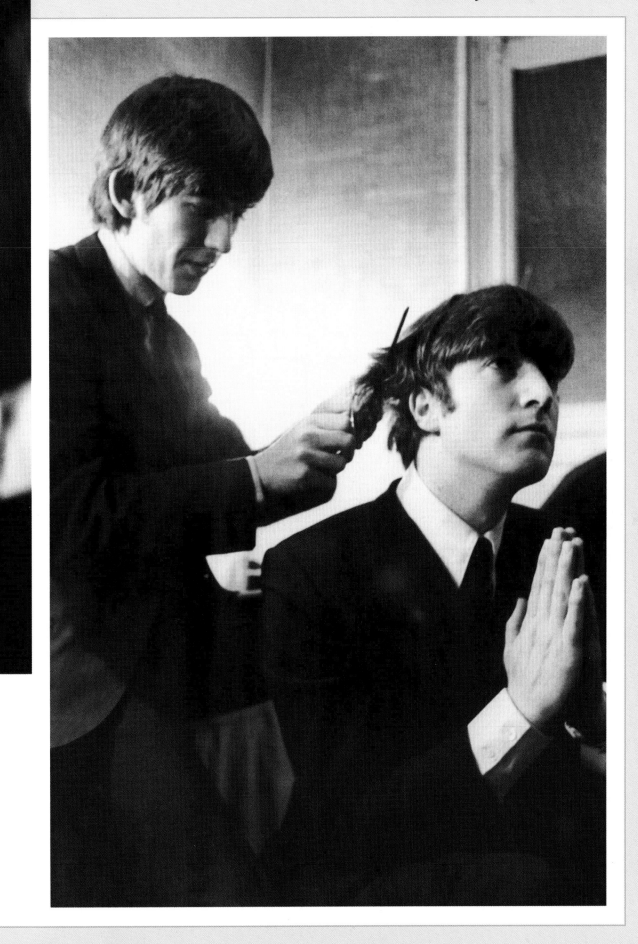

> In those early days, John was virtually the leader of the Beatles—certainly not Brian Epstein [holding the camera]. I suppose McCartney was my favorite, but closely followed by Lennon, who was undoubtedly the brightest of them all. One way to alleviate boredom was to have your mates 'round, and friends of the Beatles often dropped in to their dressing room. Actress Sandra Caron [in the hat] was a great pal, as was her sister, the singer Alma Cogan. "

“ The Beatles smoked incessantly, but cigarettes—the hard stuff came later. [Above, John with composer and entertainer Lionel Bart.] They had to eat on the run, often in lorry-drivers' cafes because otherwise they would be mobbed. From the moment they became so popular that they had to hide from their fans, there was a lot of hanging around to do. Considering how much time they spent cooped up, they got on well together. 'We have rows,' said John, 'but never serious.' ”

Discs

Can you spot the rarity? It's Bob Whitaker's notorious "butcher shot" on *Yesterday and Today,* which was quickly pulled from U.S. shelves when controversy erupted.

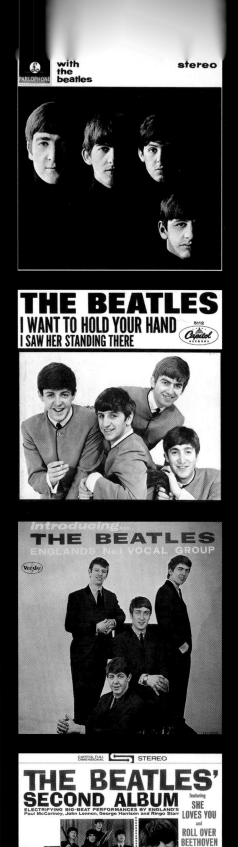

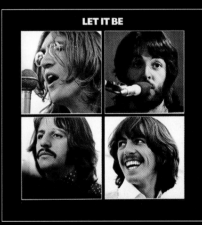

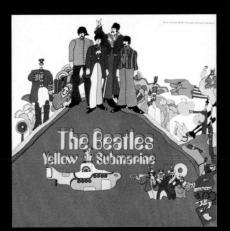

The Fab Four

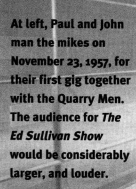

At left, Paul and John man the mikes on November 23, 1957, for their first gig together with the Quarry Men. The audience for *The Ed Sullivan Show* would be considerably larger, and louder.

Ken Regan/Camera 5

July 6, 1957. The Quarry Men are signed to play a garden fete. It's a big deal for them, and bassist Ivan Vaughan has invited a friend named Paul McCartney to the show. During a break John and Paul meet. They are quite different chaps, but they have a few things in common, one being a shared passion for music. Paul impresses John with his singing. What's more, Paul can tune a guitar, something that has thus far eluded John. Two weeks later, Paul is a Quarry Man.

The band continued to hone its skills, occasionally even in public. Before long another boy began hanging around. He was a bit younger, and thought the Quarry Men were the greatest. Eventually they let him play with them, not least because he knew a lot of chords. The boy would end up staying. His name was George Harrison.

The Quarry Men went by different names. One of them, a tribute to Buddy Holly and the Crickets, was the Silver Beatles. John changed the *e* to an *a* to play off the idea of a Beat group. By 1960 they were beginning to turn a few heads. Not many, but a few. One interested party was Allan Williams, who booked the band—now with John, Paul, George,

Pete Best on drums and John's art-school friend Stu Sutcliffe on bass—to play in Hamburg. The conditions they lived and worked in were primitive, but the experience whetted their playing to a keen edge, even as their "look" was altered by photographer Astrid Kirchherr. It was a vital period. Said John, "I was raised in Liverpool, but I grew up in Hamburg."

In mid-'61, they were in Liverpool, but without Sutcliffe, who was engaged to marry Kirchherr. Playing at an underground joint called the Cavern Club, the Beatles, as they were now called, were a tight, exciting quartet featuring John as a formidable lead singer. Kids eagerly queued up for every show. A 27-year-old Brian Epstein, who ran a music store, caught their act and sensed the buzz. Epstein became their manager and was able to secure a recording session, but with an edict from producer George Martin that Pete Best be replaced on drums by a fellow Englishman they had come to know in Hamburg, one Ringo Starr.

The die was cast. Fame and fortune were drawing nigh, and four young men from the tough port city would soon be awash in the bittersweet nectar that flows from the font of extreme fame.

K&K/Star File

Learning the Ropes

Above, in one of the various permutations of the Quarry Men, John, Paul and George are in the foreground as the band jams in Liverpool in 1960. At right, in Hamburg later that year and now called the Beatles, are (left to right) Paul, Pete Best, Stu Sutcliffe, George and John. Opposite: In 1961, John takes in the scene in Hamburg, like his hometown, a rugged port city.

The Liverpool Scene

At left, in 1959, in the Rainbow Room of a Liverpool nightspot called the Casbah Coffee Club, Paul appears to have eyes only for the young woman in the flowered dress, but she is Cynthia Powell, who has been dating John for a while and will marry him in 1962. Julian Lennon is their son. The couple divorced in 1968. Above and below, the boys play and play around at their regular Liverpool stomping grounds, the Cavern Club.

On the Cusp

These photographs, all taken at the Cavern on the night of February 19, 1963, effectively capture its subterranean quality. The Beatles will receive a bit of sensational news three days hence: Their single "Please Please Me," which was released in the U.K. on January 11, reaches the No. 1 spot on the *New Musical Express* chart.

Terence Spencer

An Early Summit Meeting

This little gathering takes place in London in 1963. Facing the camera, from left, are George, Johnny Gustafson, John, and Mick Jagger. Gustafson was a Liverpool musician who played with a few minor groups and also essayed a solo career, but he never enjoyed any appreciable success. Jagger, by contrast, was and is the front man of the Rolling Stones, self-proclaimed greatest rock band in the world. When this photo was taken, the Stones were charting with "I Wanna Be Your Man," a song that had been written by Lennon-McCartney and given to the Stones as a favor. In 1971, taking umbrage at diminishing remarks about the Beatles made by Jagger, John told *Rolling Stone* that Jagger and his group weren't "in the same class, musicwise or powerwise, never were."

Rocker and Rocker-to-be

On April 8, 1963, John Charles Julian Lennon was born to Cynthia and
John at Sefton General Hospital in Liverpool. John phoned Cynthia
from London, where he was playing with the Beatles. Here, he holds
the infant in the back garden of his Aunt Mimi's house. Over the
years, father and son had a distant, strained relationship, though they
stayed in touch. Opposite, John composes himself before a concert.

The Invasion

It is February 7, 1964, and Pan Am Flight 101 from London has just arrived at Kennedy Airport in New York City. America will never be the same. The Beatles have the No. 1 song in the land with "I Want to Hold Your Hand," and a frenzy is developing. Girls scream for them, but boys love their music too.

A Night to Remember

Two days after landing, the Beatles draw a record number of viewers when they appear on Ed Sullivan's Sunday evening TV show. The crowd shrieks in ecstasy as the boys perform a few of their current hits. Above, Sullivan and John mug it up. At right, Brian Epstein and John, Ringo and Paul look on as Sullivan comes to grips with Paul's bass. Opposite, in rehearsal.

A Veddy Brief Tour of the Colonies

Opposite: While in New York for the Sullivan show, three of the lads get to see a bit of the city. (George was under the weather and stayed in the hotel.) Here, John totes five-year-old Debra Fyall on his shoulder, while Ringo makes sure she is O.K. Above and right, on the train from New York to Washington, D.C., John takes in the scenery, then he and George compare notes on smoking.

To ferry them about for their second tour of the States in 1964, the lads chartered a Lockheed Electra from American Flyers Airline. The pilot was Reed Pigman, who had started the company in Dallas in the 1940s. To give the Beatles a break on the tour, Pigman brought them to his ranch in the Ozarks for a few days, where they went riding, hiking and played board games at night. It may be that some of the stewardesses were in attendance as well. Pigman died two years later, on April 22, 1966, when this very plane crashed.

Charles Trainor

You Can't Do That

On September 11, 1964, during the one-month tour of the U.S. and Canada, the group plays a show at the Gator Bowl, in Jacksonville, Fla. A hurricane named Dora has just preceded them, and winds are still howling, but there is yet another storm. Local authorities had threatened to segregate the audience, but John, Paul, George and Ringo—appalled by racial friction they have encountered on the tour, say they will not play unless the segregation order is withdrawn. Authorities comply. It is said that the Beatles smoked grass for the first time on this tour, in New York with Bob Dylan.

A Hard Day's Night

In 1964, the Beatles starred in their first film, which director Richard Lester shot as a typical day in their kaleidoscopic lives, replete with a sterling sound track. The iconic image at left has them fleeing their fans, very much an everyday, real-world problem. Above, in a still from the movie, John and Anna Quayle consider his image. At right, he has a bit of a larf on the set. This year also saw John go in yet another direction as he published his first book, *In His Own Write*.

Trendsetter

The Fabs were always noted
for their role in fashion trends,
and here, all within the
confines of 1964, John tries on
a few different looks. Above,
that's manager Brian Epstein
seated in the background.

Curt Gunther/London Features

Curt Gunther/MPTV

Hulton/Getty

Live and In Person

A young Italian fan has designs on John's trademark cap during this performance in Rome on June 28, 1965. Four days earlier, John's second book, *A Spaniard in the Works,* was published. It was quite Lennonesque—puns and other wordplay suffusing strange short stories and poems, all accompanied by his drawings. In the photo above, a girl is carried off by security, although she at least has the presence of mind to hang on to her purse. This show, held in Candlestick Park in San Francisco on August 29, 1966, is, incredibly, the last concert the Beatles will ever play.

AP; inset: Globe

"I'd Love to Turn You On"

John strikes a pose in 1967 in a jacket that, according to his cousin Stan Parkes, was the inspiration for the *Sgt. Pepper's* look. That psychedelic album, released on June 1 in the U.K. and the next day in the States, colored the summer as no record has before or since. Drug use by the young was becoming rampant, and John was no exception. He later said he may have taken a thousand LSD trips. At left, John listens to a playback with George Martin, the incomparable producer who was essential to that album and so many others. The lads couldn't read or write music, and it was Martin who enabled them to properly express themselves. Above, with Julian, John shows off his psychedelic Rolls-Royce.

The Inner Self

If nothing else, the Beatles were always
open to trying anything new . . . or old.
Here, in 1967, they visit with the
Maharishi Mahesh Yogi in Wales as
transcendental meditation becomes the
order of the day. In the long run, it
seemed to suit George better than the
others, although all four of them went on
a retreat to India the following year.
Above, that's Jane Asher with Paul,
Cynthia with John, Pattie with husband
George and Maureen with husband Ringo.

The Walrus Was Paul

While en route from America to England on April 11, 1967, Paul came up with the idea for something called *Magical Mystery Tour*, which would end up being a quite odd sojourn through the English countryside, with occasional music from the lads. Although all four Beatles worked on the project, it was clearly Paul at the helm. The movie debuted on BBC-TV on December 26, Boxing Day. The critics shredded the show, but the fact that it was unwisely broadcast in black and white certainly didn't help matters. Paul later said that "it wasn't the greatest thing we'd ever done. I defend it on the lines that nowhere else do you see a performance of 'I Am the Walrus.' John got the first line for that iconic song on an acid trip, and the second line a week later on another trip. He is seen here in photos taken on the set of the movie.

The Final Group Portraits

On August 22, 1969, the Beatles gathered at Tittenhurst Park, John's lovely estate near Ascot. It was the last time the four would pose together. At left, Yoko and Linda McCartney have a chat. There are many who believe that these two women were central to the band's breakup. Others say it was inevitable. In six days, Linda will give birth to Mary, her first child with Paul. She is pictured on the back of Paul's first solo album.

The Public Finale

It certainly wasn't a concert, but on January 30, 1969, the Fab Four ascended to the top of their London headquarters on a cold, blustery day and held a jam session. After about 40 minutes the police brought a halt to matters, as traffic in the capital city had been brought to a standstill. If this "show" inspired in their fans the hope that the lads were going to go on tour or some such, well, that was a hollow dream. This outing would be the last time the Beatles played together publicly.

Beatlemania!

Yeah, yeah, yeah: If you'd saved the Beatles wig and Fab Four lunchbox, you'd make a killing today on eBay. But face it, if you still had treasures from that golden time, you'd keep them forever.

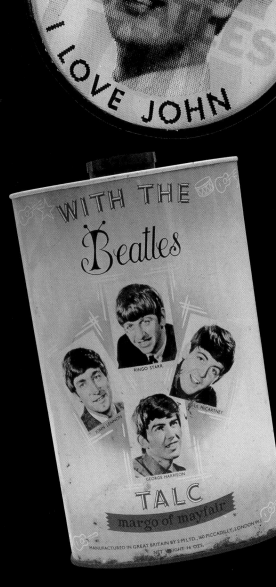

"A SECOND TIME" "HOLD ME TIGHT" "I SAW HER STANDING THERE"

"I WANT TO HOLD YOUR HAND"

THE BEATLES
© NEMS ENT. LTD

"HOLD ME TIGHT"

"DON'T BOTHER ME"

THE FABULOUS **BEATLES** JEWELLERY BROOCH

DESIGN

"BEATLES"

ASTICS LTD., LEICESTER, ENG.

RESERVED
J 17 38
$4.00

HOLLYWOOD BOWL
2301 N. Highland Ave.
HOLLYWOOD   CALIFORNIA
AUG. 23 **THE BEATLES**
1964
SAT. EVE. AUG. 23, 8:00 P.M.
PRICE $4.00
NO REFUNDS — NO EXCHANGES

THE BEATLES

24J
BOX
FIELD LEVEL BOX
SEAT 4

SHEA STADIUM
FLUSHING, N.Y.
SUNDAY
AUG. 15
1965
8:00 P.M.

SID BERNSTEIN, Presents
"THE BEATLES"
Established Price $5.00
Federal Tax   .40
City Tax   .25
TOTAL $5.65

SID BERNSTEIN, Presents

RAIN CHECK — SEE REVERSE SIDE

SUN., AUG. 15, 1965-8 P.M.
LEVEL BOX $5.65
24J BOX
SEAT 4

The **BEATLES**
JIGSAW
APPROX. SIZE 17" x 11"

THE BEATLES

FREE INSIDE! BEATLES 20-HIT SONG BOOK
Fabulous
Australia 1/6 New Zealand 1/3 South Africa 15 cents JANUARY 18th 1964
THE WORLD'S POP STARS IN COLOUR COLOUR COLOUR ALL THE WAY 1/-

Robert Whitaker *Remembers*

"In doing portraits, I usually put some objects in the photograph as a point of reference as to who or what the subject is," says Bob Whitaker, asked to remember a day in Melbourne in 1964, when he was a young English photographer working abroad. "With him, I put peacock feathers around his head. He loved the idea, then went to see an exhibition I had up at the time. He asked me if I wanted to return to London and work for him."

The subject of the session was not John Lennon or any of the other Beatles, who were on a tour Down Under. It was the band's manager, peacocky Brian Epstein. At first, Whitaker demurred. "Then Brian said, 'Well, come see the Beatles at Royal Festival Hall.' I got shoved into the orchestra pit, so I was right between the Beatles playing their music and these girls just screaming and fainting away. I couldn't hear a damn thing, but I could see these girls and I thought, 'I suppose I'm missing out on something here.'" Sooner rather than later, Whitaker was back in London, photographing Cilla Black, Gerry & the Pacemakers and others in Epstein's stable—most prominently, of course, the Beatles.

"I found it actually quite difficult to become part of the group," recalls Whitaker, the band's official photographer until 1966. "I didn't talk music. Paul seemed to sneer when I'd point a camera his way. Ringo was always a great wit, and could cope fantastically, but we weren't very close. It was John I felt quite at home with, and we got to be very friendly. We'd talk about Dalí or Magritte or other painters. We used to paint together, discussing odd things—the solidity of objects here and in space. I think that one had a bit to do with LSD.

"I found John humorous, warm, very witty. His art—the drawings and poetry—is humorous beyond belief. Very Spike Milligan, but also beautiful. All four were very inventive and spontaneous. On a tour around England in 1964, we were up in Argyllshire at this country house and I asked them to jump up on a wall there. They grabbed these umbrellas, and then John . . . well, look at him in that photo. He's *levitating.*"

> **Once I started with them, I realized right away that shooting the Beatles wasn't the sort of work I was used to doing, which was fashion photography, working with photomontage, other odd things. I think that's why John liked how some of it turned out—it was different.**

> " I had been studying the Greek myth of Narcissus, and one day at the Lennons', I got John to look at his reflection in the water. I had him put a dandelion over his eye. Then I gave John a hoe and Cynthia a mop, and tried to turn them into something very real: pioneers. We shoved a gold spoon into Julian's hand. I thought the three of them were a fabulous family. I never discussed with John why he left Cynthia. "

> Portraiture of four Beatles gleaming their white teeth at you bored me senseless. So I was lucky because wherever they were, I was part of the party. I was fascinated to hear them play backstage—this was in Germany, either Hamburg or Essen or Munich—to hear them singing in tune. Onstage, you couldn't hear a thing. A lot of these photos never ran back then because the papers wanted all four boys: John-Paul-George-Ringo was one person. And a lot of the best moments, of course, had only one Beatle. Or two. Or three.

“ The whiskers were for *Help!* The mask? It was '66. They were prisoners in the Tokyo Hilton but wanted to see things. So merchants brought lacquer boxes, masks, anything Japanese. John's moment with the mask was utterly spontaneous. We were in America—Houston or Minneapolis or Portland—when the cat licked John's nose, and he started stroking it. Very much him. I never saw John as a hard bastard at all. Never saw him bite, or be disrespectful. I miss him a great deal. ”

Bob Gruen *Remembers*

Chuck Pulin

"I didn't know the Beatles," says Bob Gruen simply. "I knew John." And Gruen knew him in the 1970s, having met Lennon and Yoko Ono in the spring of '72 when he was assigned to shoot their backup band, Elephant's Memory. "We got along really well, and I started spending more time with them. At the time, they were living in Greenwich Village on Bank Street, right near me.

"I found John to be very much as expected—open, witty, perceptive. He would tell these funny one-liners, and I always had

a good time with him—a lot of fun. Yoko, too. John would never marry a humorless person, and there was a lot of laughter around them. People ask me what kind of woman Yoko is, and I answer, 'The kind John Lennon would marry.' "

In the 1970s, Gruen chronicled the rock scene in New York City, and while his work sometimes took him elsewhere, the Gotham nightlife offered plenty to shoot at home. "I was macho-proud of New York and was glad John loved the city too. I had a half dozen of the NEW YORK T-shirts, and I gave John one. I didn't give it to him to wear for those photos, I gave it to him a year earlier. He still had it when we made those pictures.

"Later, when he and Yoko were sort of in seclusion, we were still in touch. They'd ask me to come uptown to take photos of Sean. John was very protective of Sean as a baby, and those pictures were just for them—they didn't circulate at the time.

"My pictures of them were spontaneous moments. That's how it was: John always lived for the moment. Once, a guy in Central Park yelled, 'When you getting back with the Beatles?' John yelled back, 'When you going back to high school?' When he was ready to come out in public again in 1980, I gave him videos of the newer bands and asked him if he wanted to go to the clubs and see some of them. He said, 'I've been there. Same thing as Hamburg. I know what that's like.' He wasn't one to look back."

" In 1974 we did the NEW YORK CITY T-shirt shots, with and without the denim jacket. I prefer the one with just the T-shirt [seen on the back cover of this book] and I think John did as well. It's my best-known picture. John feeding Sean [left] was taken at the Dakota in November of 1975. "

Bob Gruen *Remembers*

"These were two house-hunting shots from spring, 1973. One is of John and Yoko walking in the rain near Central Park, before taking a first look at the Dakota apartment. The other one is on a pond in Greenwich, Connecticut, at—believe it or not—my former mother-in-law's house. I had driven them up there in an old station wagon. They bought in the city, of course."

“ John said he loved New York because the artists and creativity of the world were here. He said if it was during the Roman Empire, he'd live in Rome. That's Elton John on piano at the Record Plant in 1974, and Andy Warhol, same place, in '72. Phil Spector [in the hat] made an album of John's benefit concert at Madison Square Garden in 1972. ”

They're dancing at about eight a.m. at the Hit Factory Studio in the fall of 1980. They've just heard "Starting Over" for the first time on the radio, and after a whole night in the studio, they just started dancing—they were so happy. The others are also from the Hit Factory, the *Double Fantasy* sessions. I love John explaining it all to Sean. He was always looking to the future.

Discs

There's a controversial cover here, too: They're naked under the brown wrapping of *Two Virgins*. John, when he was a boy, created the art that graces *Walls and Bridges*.

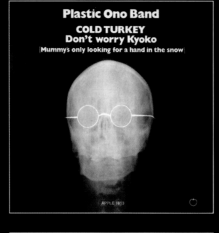

John & Yoko

At left, very near the end, the Beatles, George Martin and Yoko Ono listen to a tape during the making of the *Let It Be* album. Here, Yoko and John in 1969.

April 10, 1970. The Beatles issue a statement saying, "The world is still spinning and so are we and so are you. When the spinning stops—that'll be the time to worry. Not before. The Beatles are alive and well and the beat goes on. The beat goes on."

Well, maybe the beat went on, but without the Beatles. The message above, sent through their company, Apple, was an obituary notice, whether anyone knew it or not. The most popular and influential group in musical history would be no more. Friction had been increasing for a long time. Harsh words had been exchanged. The otherworldly heat and exposure that came from being a Beatle was proving too much for anyone to handle—especially John. The regimen of it had become something like school—thus, it was a thing he knew he needed to be free of.

In the spring of 1968, he fell in love with a performance artist he had met a couple of years earlier. Seven years his elder, Yoko Ono would release John from the "shackles" of Beatledom. She, more than a maharishi or LSD, opened John's eyes to a different way of living—one in which he didn't have to hang out with bandmates every day. Instead, he would hang out with her. Barring one breakup that lasted a little over a year, the two were inseparable for as long as John lived.

It was Paul who personally called for an end to the Beatles in April 1970, tying it to the release of his solo album. But John and Yoko had already released four albums of their own, and George was working on his own musical things too. It was all, finally, just so inevitable, even though George and Ringo said at the time that each was confident the group would work together again. This, of course, was not to be.

John's first post-Beatles LP was *Plastic Ono Band,* an unflinching, brutally honest album that bored deep into his anger, fear and disillusionment. Similar themes were explored on his next record, the classic *Imagine.* For the remainder of his career he produced works that were mainly serious explorations of serious issues: politics, religion, war, and often his complex relationship with Yoko. Ironically, the music that John frequently turned to was the straightforward stuff of his youth. "I like rock 'n' roll," he once said. "I don't like much else."

David Nutter/Camera Press/Retna

The Wedding Bed

Yoko was born in Tokyo in 1933 to a family of bankers and socialites who relocated in 1952 to Scarsdale, N.Y., a wealthy suburb north of New York City. When she met John in 1966, there was a dynamism between the two that would not be denied. Three years later, on March 20, 1969, above, John and Yoko make it official when they are married in Gibralter in a 10-minute ceremony. For a honeymoon, they head for Amsterdam, where, at right, a weeklong bed-in for peace at the Hilton attracts enormous attention. Eight days earlier, in another shocker, Paul had married American photographer Linda Eastman.

Seeing the Sights

Above, in Scotland in 1969, John and Yoko escort Julian and Kyoko, Yoko's daughter. The girl came from Yoko's second marriage, to Tony Cox (1962–1969), who had custody of the child. This trip was marred when a car accident left John, Yoko and the kids in a hospital for the better part of a week. Opposite: The next year, again on holiday with Kyoko, this time in Denmark, John carries Yoko across the frozen turf.

Look at Me

Above, on December 11, 1968, John and Yoko
are on the set of *The Rolling Stones: Rock
and Roll Circus,* a television project that
wasn't released until 1996. Along with fire
eaters, clowns and trapeze artists, such acts
as The Who and Jethro Tull played—and, of
course, the Stones. John appeared with
some other rock superstars (Eric Clapton,
Keith Richards, Mitch Mitchell) in a group
dubbed The Dirty Mac. Their first of two
songs was a rendition of "Yer Blues" from
the White Album; then came something
called "Whole Lotta Yoko," in which she
wails and keens as the group backs her. At
right, on February 12, 1970. Far right, in their
West Village home in New York in 1971, the
husband and wife engage in Bagism.
Created by them, Bagism is an art form that,
perhaps, attempts to prevent others from
making generalizations based on physical
characteristics. As a cultural contribution, it
doesn't quite rank with "A Day in the Life."

Working Class Hero

Above, just like any other English couple cast in a
domestic setting in 1971, except that this is Yoko
and John, and they are at his splendiferous estate,
Tittenhurst Park. Opposite: On August 30, 1972, they
perform at the One to One Concert at Madison Square
Garden. John and Yoko play more than a dozen songs
in the show, a benefit for handicapped children at
Willowbrook, a state school in Staten Island, N.Y.

Harry Goodwin/Star File

The Lost Weekend

At left, John shares a table with May Pang in 1974. At the time, he was estranged from Yoko and was seeing Pang, Yoko's former secretary. John was spending most of his time in California, and was on a serious bender. He later told *Playboy* that, without Yoko, "I was on a raft alone in the middle of the universe . . . It was the lost weekend that lasted 18 months. I've never drunk so much in my life. I tried to drown myself in the bottle and I was with the heaviest drinkers in the business . . . Harry Nilsson, Bobby Keyes, Keith Moon." Above, Nilsson and John playing pool. At right, a bouncer ejects Nilsson and John from a club in West Hollywood for loudly heckling at a performance by the Smothers Brothers.

A Family Man

After his period of debauchery, John returned to Yoko for good, and with the birth of their son, Sean, on October 9, 1975, John became a dyed-in-the-wool homebody for several years. During this time he very much stayed away from the music scene. He said that he considered Sean his first son, in the sense that he was "a planned child," although he emphasized that he loved Julian, and always would. This is Sean in all these pictures. At left, Daddy gives the boy important shaving tips in their apartment in the Dakota building in New York City, September 1980.

Paul Goresh

Strawberry Fields Forever

December 8, 1980. The creative juices are flowing through John as he heads out for a productive session in the studio. Outside the Dakota, he is stopped, above, by a man named Mark David Chapman, a longtime "fan" who asks John to sign a copy of *Double Fantasy*. At 10:50 that night, when John and Yoko come home, Chapman emerges from the shadows calling out, "Mr. Lennon," and shoots John dead. Below, a mosaic in the nearby section of Central Park that is christened Strawberry Fields. At right, mourners gather in the park.

David LeFranc/Gamma

Ken Sherman

Allan Tannenbaum *Remembers*

Harry Mattison

sions for rock music and photography by shooting the cultural scene, first in San Francisco and then in New York City. Throughout the '70s he chronicled anything that was happening in the Big Apple—from City Hall to the Mudd Club—for the *SoHo Weekly News*. When he learned, in late 1980, that John and Yoko were about to emerge from five years of virtual seclusion to promote a new album, the *SoHo News* made an overture—and thus began, tentatively at first, a series of photo sessions that yielded a remarkable portfolio. "It all happened over a couple days in late November," says Tannenbaum. "I reviewed the pictures with John and Yoko because I wanted to make them some prints. John would say, 'I like this one, I like that one.' He joked that one of the big problems with the Beatles had been that they all liked different shots best.

"I made prints, and on December 8, I was going to take them up to the Dakota. I was running a bit late when I got the call telling me what had happened. Everything changed right then. Everything."

> It was a brilliantly sunny fall day and they were being filmed for a video, visiting some of their favorite places in Central Park. John was wearing this silver jacket. I took my still pictures. After we did those shots, we had some coffee and Yoko said, 'John is comfortable with you.' So there would be other opportunities.

He has covered the Intifada in the Middle East and also the first Gulf War. He has made *Time* cover photos of such as Oliver North and Ariel Sharon. He has twice—in 1993 and on September 11, 2001—raced with his cameras from his Manhattan apartment to cover terrorist attacks at the World Trade Center. And yet the photojournalist Allan Tannenbaum says, "Those photos of John and Yoko represent one of the most significant moments not only in my career but in my life. They're as important to me as any pictures I've made."

That's because of who Tannenbaum is—what matters to him, what informed his upbringing and philosophy—and because of events that unfolded soon after Tannenbaum's short but intimate association with John and Yoko began.

"In the '60s I was a big Beatles and Stones fan," he says. "I couldn't decide which band I liked better. With the Beatles, I was a John guy. I liked his style, his humor, especially his outspokenness." After graduating from college in 1967 with an art degree, Tannenbaum was able to combine his pas-

Polaris

In their office in the Dakota they were full of energy and excitement: They were coming out again, they were planning to tour, they were excited. They clearly loved each other, and there was a lot of give and take. Yoko could be businesslike and full of ideas, but John was not at all passive. He'd be playful and humor her, saying 'Yes, Mother,' when she gave directions. That day, I felt like a fly on the wall.

" Our last session was at a downtown studio made to look like their bedroom. I remember going over the shots later with John and he said, 'You know what I like about your photos? They make Yoko look so beautiful.' It made me so happy. It still cuts me after all these years. Twenty-five years—it's like the blink of an eye. Shocking, just shocking. We lost a real humanist, a cultural icon. And a New Yorker. "

Harry Benson *Remembers*

John Lennon

One photographer was there at the beginning, and after the end. Benson was a native Scotsman working as a young newspaperman on London's Fleet Street when, "on January 13, 1964, to be exact, the night desk editor called to say I was to go to Paris the next day with a new pop group. I was all packed—had gotten the necessary shots—to leave the next day for Nairobi. Thinking myself a serious photojournalist, I told him, 'No, thanks, I'm off to Africa.' Five minutes later the phone rang again: 'The editor says you are going to Paris.' "

Harry did, of course, go to France where he covered, first, a performance at the Cyrano Theatre in Versailles. "I had to go out to my car to get batteries for my strobe. When I got back inside the hall, I heard the strains, 'Close your eyes and I'll kiss you, tomorrow I'll miss you . . .' It was the first Beatles' song I'd ever heard, and it was sensational. The moment I heard them, I knew I was in the right place."

Benson stayed in that place—right by the Beatles' side—in those headiest of days, as they conquered Europe and invaded America. Years later, as it happened, Benson was already a longtime resident of New York City . . . on the night tragedy struck.

> **In Paris they had a beautiful suite in the George V. It had a large living room with a piano where they'd play and compose. My room down the hall had two big beds. George slept there a few nights as the others were partying so late. John took that picture of me [above] as a Beatle.**

On the Pan Am plane on February 7, 1964, everyone was excited yet apprehensive about coming to America. It had been just over two months since JFK was assassinated, and that was very much on their minds. Eerily, John said that he feared an Ivy League guy in a suit would try to kill him. It was the first trip to America for John and Cynthia, who were subdued on the plane. John and George took pictures of everyone to pass time. I was the fifth person off the plane, and I had asked them to turn around and wave. Ringo remembered and made the others turn. I didn't bother to develop the film until about 15 years later. I'm glad I finally did, as it was an historic day. After New York, we took the train to Washington. Someone made Cynthia wear a black wig [opposite, bottom], ostensibly so fans wouldn't mob her. She was actually kept aside so as not to hurt John's image. The Beatles were desperate to succeed, and Cynthia was a casualty of that agenda. She never rode in the limo, always followed in the second car. It was sad.

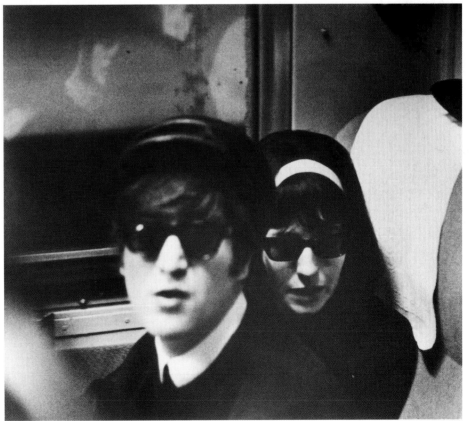

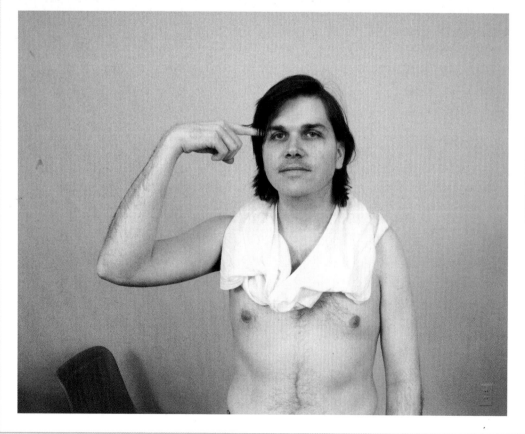

In 1966, when Lennon's 'We're more popular than Jesus Christ' interview was published in America, all hell broke loose. I found out John would be giving a press conference in Chicago. After his public apology, I found him in his hotel room, smoking, almost in tears. 'Why couldn't I keep my big mouth shut?' In 1980, when I heard that John had been shot, I was stunned like everyone else.

For a short part of my life, he had been a friend. Many fans gathered in Central Park on December 14 to mourn the loss of their idol. His songs were played and for a moment a sign with a photograph of John and the word WHY? arose from the crowd. Then it was gone. Much later, in 1987, it was arranged that I would take pictures of Mark David Chapman for a magazine article. It was in Attica, a

grim old prison. The editor told Chapman of my history with the Beatles and he was intrigued. Touching my arm, he said, 'I want to apologize to you for killing your friend.' But then, when I was photographing him, the last thing he did was put a finger to his temple like he was holding a revolver. All in all—thinking back—it seemed like one incredible hour with a madman.

" I had heard many things about Yoko Ono, of course, but we had never met before I first photographed her and Sean in 1985. When I photographed them at the Imagine Circle in Central Park, she told me that she and Sean had to go on living—John would have wanted it that way. I found her to be a charming, intelligent woman—and it was easy to see why John had been in love with her. I hadn't met her earlier because, you see, I wasn't a rock 'n' roll photographer. I had covered the Beatles as a news story, a phenomenal news story. I remember, by the time they got to Boston for their performance at Suffolk Downs racetrack on August 18, 1966, the world-weariness had set in. John remarked that they had seen America from inside hotel rooms and from looking out of car windows. It was obvious they would not do any more world tours and, afterwards, I went my own way, and they went theirs. The last time I saw John was in the late '60s in New York's Bryant Park. He was at a peace rally protesting the Vietnam War, where he said, 'All we are saying is: Give peace a chance.' "

Just One More

The Night Dreamt Of . . . The Night When Everything Changed

Every life is made up of moments—quiet ones, raucous ones, moments long sought and moments too quickly past. It could be said that this was *the* moment for all four of them—certainly for John, who had, ever since hearing "Heartbreak Hotel," desperately wanted the golden ring. Harry Benson was there that night, too, at the George V in Paris, and tells LIFE: "It was late, and Brian Epstein came in with a cable to tell them 'I Want to Hold Your Hand' was No. 1 on the American charts, and that they were going to America to be on *The Ed Sullivan Show*. They were obviously excited by the news. I had heard them talk about a pillow fight they had had earlier, and I suggested one that night. Three said O.K., but John said no—that would be childish and stupid. So that was that. Then John casually came up behind Paul, who was holding a drink in his hand, and whacked him across the head. That was when the fun began."